I0011976

Digital Burnout: Overcoming the Mental and Physical Toll of the Digital Age

Practical Strategies for Reclaiming Balance, Rebuilding Emotional Resilience, and Managing Technology Overload

Introduction: Navigating Digital Burnout in the Age of Constant Connectivity

In today's fast-paced, hyper-connected world, digital burnout has emerged as a significant challenge for individuals across various age groups and professions. With the constant influx of notifications, emails, messages, and social media updates, it's no surprise that many people are feeling overwhelmed and mentally drained. The digital age has revolutionized the way we live, work, and communicate, but it has also introduced a new set of stressors that can lead to mental, emotional, and physical exhaustion. Digital burnout, a term that refers to the exhaustion and detachment caused by overexposure to technology, is now a widespread issue that affects everything from personal well-being to productivity and work-life balance.

The demand to always be "on" – constantly checking devices, responding to work emails, and staying updated on social media – has created a 24/7 culture where relaxation and downtime are often sacrificed. This relentless pressure can take a toll on one's mental health, leaving individuals feeling disengaged, unfocused, and emotionally drained. Whether you're a professional trying to keep up with emails and deadlines, a student navigating the challenges of remote learning, or an individual seeking to maintain a healthy social media presence, digital burnout is an issue that knows no boundaries.

This book seeks to explore the causes, symptoms, and solutions to digital burnout, helping readers understand the root of this growing concern and providing practical strategies to regain balance in a technology-driven world. Through research-backed insights, real-world examples, and actionable tips, you will learn how to manage your digital life in a way that promotes mental well-being, productivity, and overall satisfaction. By understanding the effects of overuse and developing healthy digital habits, you can break free from the cycle of digital exhaustion and create a more balanced, fulfilling lifestyle.

In this book, we will uncover the impact of excessive screen time on mental health, explore the connection between technology and stress, and discuss how to establish boundaries in an always-connected world. You'll discover methods for managing technology use effectively, identifying signs of digital burnout before it becomes overwhelming, and finding ways to reclaim control over your digital life. Whether you're struggling with burnout or simply seeking to optimize your relationship with technology, this guide will provide you with the tools you need to navigate the challenges of the digital age and embrace a healthier, more mindful approach to connectivity.

By the end of this book, you'll be empowered with the knowledge and strategies to combat digital burnout, protect your mental health, and find a harmonious balance between the digital world and your personal life. Welcome to the journey of reclaiming your time, your energy, and your peace of mind in a digitally-driven world.

Chapter 1: The Digital Age and Its Toll

In the digital age, technology has become inseparable from everyday life. From the moment we wake up to the moment we go to sleep, we are constantly plugged into a world of smartphones, social media, emails, and a 24/7 stream of information. While this connectivity has undoubtedly brought numerous conveniences, it has also introduced new challenges, including the rise of digital burnout. As we navigate a world increasingly dominated by screens, it's important to understand the toll technology takes on our mental, emotional, and physical well-being.

The Rise of Smartphones, Social Media, and Constant Connectivity

The proliferation of smartphones and social media platforms has fundamentally reshaped the way we communicate, work, and interact with others. In a world where notifications are constant, it's difficult to unplug, even for a few minutes. The average person checks their phone more than 100 times a day, with the majority of these interactions involving notifications from apps, emails, or social media. With constant access to information, the lines between work and personal life have become increasingly blurred. Remote work, while offering flexibility, has also introduced the expectation of being available around the clock. Whether it's responding to work emails after hours or staying active on social media, technology is now an omnipresent force that demands our attention at all times.

The rise of social media platforms has further compounded the situation. While social media offers an avenue for connection and expression, it can also contribute to stress and burnout. The constant comparison to others, the pressure to maintain an idealized online persona, and the influx of negative news can lead to feelings of inadequacy, anxiety, and fatigue. Social media is designed to keep users engaged, often leading to endless scrolling and a sense of being "always on."

Effects: The Overwhelming Presence of Technology and Its Psychological Consequences

The overwhelming presence of technology in every facet of our lives has far-reaching psychological consequences. One of the most significant impacts of digital overload is the toll it takes on mental health. Research has shown that excessive screen time, particularly on social media, is linked to increased levels of anxiety, depression, and loneliness. The constant barrage of information and notifications can lead to feelings of stress and mental exhaustion, leaving individuals feeling emotionally drained.

The phenomenon of "always-on" culture is a contributing factor to digital burnout. When individuals feel the need to be constantly available and responsive, they experience a lack of control over their time and mental space. This leads to feelings of burnout, where individuals struggle to meet the demands placed on them, often sacrificing self-care, rest, and relaxation. Over time, this can contribute to a decrease in productivity, creativity, and overall well-being.

The physical toll of technology overuse is equally concerning. Prolonged screen time can lead to eye strain, headaches, and poor posture, contributing to physical discomfort. Additionally, the constant stimulation from digital devices can disrupt sleep patterns, leading to sleep deprivation and fatigue. The negative impact on sleep quality can further exacerbate feelings of burnout, creating a vicious cycle.

Statistics: The Growing Prevalence of Digital Burnout

The rise of digital burnout is not just anecdotal; it is a growing concern backed by research. According to a 2023 survey by the American Psychological Association, nearly 60% of adults report experiencing symptoms of burnout, with technology use being one of the primary contributors. In particular, individuals who spend more than 6 hours a day on screens report higher levels of stress, anxiety, and dissatisfaction with life.

A 2022 study by the World Health Organization (WHO) found that 1 in 4 employees experience burnout, with those working in technology-driven industries being at a higher risk. The study noted that the constant pressure to be connected, along with the expectation of rapid responses, creates a perfect storm for digital burnout.

In the U.S., a 2023 report from the Pew Research Center found that 46% of adults felt overwhelmed by the amount of information they were expected to process daily, with 65% of those individuals citing the overwhelming nature of digital communication as a significant stressor. In fact, more than half of workers report feeling unable to disconnect from work due to the pervasiveness of digital communication, leading to increased levels of stress and anxiety.

These statistics highlight the growing prevalence of digital burnout and the urgent need for individuals to address their relationship with technology. As we continue to immerse ourselves in a digital world, understanding the psychological consequences of overuse becomes crucial in reclaiming balance and mental well-being.

Chapter 2: What Is Digital Burnout?

In the era of digital connectivity, many of us find ourselves overwhelmed by the very tools designed to make our lives easier. As we navigate our daily routines, it's becoming increasingly difficult to escape the constant buzz of notifications, emails, and social media updates. Digital burnout has emerged as a serious condition, affecting people from all walks of life. But what exactly is digital burnout, and how does it differ from traditional burnout? In this chapter, we will explore the deeper emotional and mental impact of this modern phenomenon, its symptoms, and real-world stories from individuals who are struggling with it.

Definition: A Deeper Understanding of Digital Burnout

Digital burnout is a mental, emotional, and physical state of exhaustion that occurs as a result of excessive and overwhelming digital engagement. It goes beyond simply feeling tired from a long day of work or screen time; it is the profound fatigue and stress caused by the constant demand for attention from digital devices. Digital burnout occurs when an individual's need for rest and detachment from technology is ignored, leading to mental depletion, emotional exhaustion, and an inability to "switch off."

This modern form of burnout is characterized by the unrelenting pressure to stay connected, respond to messages and emails quickly, and maintain an active presence on social media. In contrast to traditional burnout, which is often linked to work-related stress and physical exhaustion, digital burnout is unique in that it is directly tied to technology. It is a modern affliction that stems from an overwhelming sense of always being "on," which can lead to significant mental health challenges.

Symptoms: Fatigue, Irritability, Anxiety, Stress, and the Inability to Disconnect

Digital burnout manifests in a variety of emotional, psychological, and physical symptoms. The following are some of the most common signs that an individual may be experiencing digital burnout:

- **Fatigue**: One of the most prominent symptoms of digital burnout is constant fatigue. Even after a full night's rest, individuals may feel mentally drained and unable to keep up with their tasks. This tiredness is not physical but rather cognitive and emotional exhaustion from the overstimulation of constant digital interactions.

- **Irritability**: The constant demands of technology can lead to frustration and irritability. When people feel overwhelmed by the constant influx of notifications and messages, it can become difficult to focus, leading to shorter tempers and increased frustration in both personal and professional environments.

- **Anxiety**: Digital burnout often manifests as anxiety, particularly about staying connected and keeping up with the demands of technology. A heightened sense of urgency around responding to emails, checking social media, or managing work tasks can create persistent worry about missing out or falling behind.

- **Stress**: As the digital demands on an individual's time increase, stress levels also rise. The pressure to respond to messages instantly, keep up with social media trends, and maintain professional relationships online can feel overwhelming. This stress is compounded by the pressure to be always available, leaving individuals with little to no time to unwind.

- **The Inability to Disconnect**: One of the most alarming symptoms of digital burnout is the inability to truly disconnect from digital devices. The boundary between work and personal life becomes increasingly blurred, especially in remote work environments. Individuals may find themselves checking emails after hours, scrolling through social media in the middle of the night, or feeling the compulsion to respond to every notification. This constant state of connectivity makes it nearly impossible to unwind and recharge.

Personal Stories: Testimonies from Individuals Affected by Digital Burnout

1. *Maria's* *Story*: Maria, a marketing professional, found herself caught in a cycle of nonstop digital engagement. "I was always on my phone – checking emails, responding to messages, and scrolling through social media. Even during dinner with my family, I'd have my phone beside me, responding to work

queries. Over time, I started to feel drained. I couldn't relax. I was irritable, tired, and couldn't sleep. I knew something was wrong, but I couldn't figure out how to break free from the constant digital demands."

Maria's experience is a reflection of how digital burnout can creep into every aspect of life, from personal relationships to professional productivity.

2. *David's* *Story*:

David, a freelance writer, often found himself overwhelmed by the need to be constantly online to maintain his business. "I had the pressure of writing articles while also managing my website, responding to clients, and staying active on social media to promote my work. I thought I was handling it fine at first, but eventually, I started experiencing extreme anxiety. I felt like I had to be available all the time. I was always checking my phone, even when I was supposed to be off work. It wasn't just about the work anymore – it was about the fear of missing out on something important."

David's story highlights how the pressure to always be present in the digital world can create a sense of anxiety and stress that goes far beyond the task at hand.

3. *Sophia's Story*: Sophia, a college student, found herself drowning in digital distractions. "With online classes, social media, and constant texting, I felt like I couldn't focus on anything. I'd be studying, but every few minutes I'd check my phone. Then, I'd get lost in an Instagram feed or feel overwhelmed by my group chat. My mind was always racing, and it was hard to shut off. I wasn't sleeping well either. It was like my brain couldn't escape the digital noise, even when I wanted to relax." Sophia's experience shows how digital

burnout can also affect students and anyone who spends prolonged periods of time engaged with technology.

These personal stories reflect the real and tangible effects of digital burnout. Each individual's experience is unique, but the common thread is the overwhelming pressure to remain digitally engaged, which takes a severe toll on mental health and overall well-being.

Chapter 3: The Causes of Digital Burnout

Digital burnout doesn't occur overnight. It is a complex condition that develops gradually, fueled by a combination of factors that make it increasingly difficult to disconnect from technology. In this chapter, we will explore the key causes of digital burnout, including constant connectivity, information overload, social media addiction, and the pervasive "always-on" mentality of modern work culture. Understanding these causes is crucial in recognizing the root of digital burnout and taking steps to prevent or mitigate it.

Constant Connectivity: The Blurring of Lines Between Work and Personal Life

In the digital age, the lines between work and personal life have become increasingly blurred. Email, instant messaging, and social media have created an environment where we are expected to be constantly reachable, no matter the time or place. The ubiquity of smartphones has made it nearly impossible to fully disengage from work or social obligations.

With the rise of remote work and the widespread use of collaboration tools like Slack, Microsoft Teams, and Zoom, employees are expected to be available for communication at all hours. Notifications for work emails, urgent messages from clients, and collaboration requests from coworkers can intrude on personal time, leading to a sense of never being "off the clock." This constant connectivity fosters a feeling of obligation to respond immediately to messages, even if they come during evenings, weekends, or vacations. Over time, this lack of separation between work and personal life leads to feelings of overwhelm and burnout.

Moreover, social media platforms have made it easier to stay connected to friends, family, and colleagues, but they also encourage the expectation of constant engagement. Whether it's responding to messages on Facebook or keeping up with posts on Instagram, this constant connectivity has become a source of stress, preventing individuals from truly "switching off."

Information Overload: The Overwhelming Amount of Information We Consume Daily and Its Cognitive Impact

Every day, we are bombarded with an overwhelming amount of information from a variety of digital sources: news websites, social media platforms, email, advertisements, and more. This constant influx of data can create a sense of information overload, making it difficult to process everything we encounter and leading to cognitive fatigue.

On average, a person is exposed to around 34 gigabytes of information daily, which is more than our brains can effectively process. Constant exposure to this volume of data can cause decision fatigue, as the brain becomes overwhelmed by the sheer number of choices and stimuli. Research has shown that consuming large quantities of information without sufficient time to process it leads to stress and reduced mental clarity. This is particularly problematic in the workplace, where professionals are expected to juggle multiple tasks, emails, and messages at once.

The impact of information overload is also evident on social media, where constant updates, trending topics, and notifications create a sense of urgency to keep up. The pressure to stay informed and engaged can be mentally taxing, contributing to burnout. The result is a feeling of being mentally drained, unable to focus, and even emotionally detached due to the sheer volume of information that demands attention.

Social Media Addiction: The Pressure to Be Constantly Active on Platforms and the Comparison Culture That It Fosters

Social media addiction has become one of the primary drivers of digital burnout, particularly among younger generations. Platforms like Instagram, Facebook, Twitter, and TikTok have designed their interfaces to keep users engaged, using algorithms that show personalized content and notifications that encourage constant interaction. As a result, people spend hours scrolling, liking, commenting, and posting, often without realizing the negative impact this has on their mental health.

The pressure to maintain an active presence on social media is a significant contributor to digital burnout. Whether it's keeping up with the latest trends, posting curated images, or engaging with followers, the pressure to be constantly visible and involved on social media can be overwhelming. This constant need for validation—

through likes, comments, and shares—can create feelings of inadequacy and anxiety.

Moreover, social media often fosters a culture of comparison, where users compare their lives to the idealized versions presented by others. This comparison culture can lead to low self-esteem, depression, and feelings of isolation. The pressure to present a perfect, curated image online can be emotionally draining, leading to burnout and disengagement from both the digital world and the real world.

Digital Work Culture: The "Always-On" Mentality in the Workplace and Its Role in Exacerbating Burnout

In today's fast-paced, technology-driven work culture, the "always-on" mentality has become the norm. The expectation to be available at all times, whether for work-related communication or collaboration, is exacerbating burnout. This expectation is particularly evident in industries that rely on digital communication platforms, such as tech, marketing, and customer service.

With the advent of email, instant messaging, and collaborative project management tools, workers are under pressure to be responsive at all hours. This has led to a shift in expectations where productivity is no longer measured by hours worked but by the speed of response. When individuals are expected to reply to emails or messages immediately, or be present for virtual meetings at any time, it fosters an environment where "off-time" becomes non-existent. Even outside of work hours, employees may feel compelled to respond to work-related messages, leading to stress and burnout.

The rise of remote work has further amplified this issue. While remote work offers flexibility, it also blurs the boundaries between personal life and work life. Without a physical separation between the two, many remote workers struggle to "switch off" after work, leading to longer hours and reduced mental well-being.

Furthermore, the growing use of virtual meetings has increased the cognitive load on workers. The constant need to be on camera and participate in video calls can cause mental fatigue, especially when meetings are frequent or poorly structured. In a virtual environment, workers may also feel pressured to be "always available" on platforms like Zoom, Teams, or Slack, contributing to digital burnout.

Chapter 4: The Psychological Impact of Digital Burnout

The constant bombardment of digital stimuli—whether from work emails, social media notifications, or the endless cycle of online content—has profound effects on mental, emotional, and cognitive health. Digital burnout is not just about feeling tired or overwhelmed; it extends far deeper, affecting an individual's psychological well-being in ways that are often overlooked. This chapter explores the psychological toll of digital burnout, focusing on mental health issues, emotional exhaustion, and cognitive decline. By understanding these impacts, we can begin to take steps toward healing and recovery.

Mental Health Issues: Stress, Anxiety, Depression, and Cognitive Overload as Consequences of Constant Digital Engagement

The digital age has brought about an unprecedented level of connectivity, but with it has come a dramatic increase in stress and anxiety. The overwhelming presence of digital notifications, emails, and social media updates constantly signals to the brain that there is something demanding attention. Over time, this ceaseless mental engagement can lead to heightened stress levels and contribute to feelings of anxiety.

Research has shown that individuals who are consistently engaged with their devices, especially social media, are at higher risk of experiencing mental health issues, such as anxiety and depression. The pressure to be constantly connected, coupled with the fear of missing out (FOMO), exacerbates these feelings. Social media, in particular, fosters an environment where users compare themselves to others, which can trigger negative emotions such as inadequacy, low self-esteem, and even despair.

In addition to emotional distress, constant digital engagement leads to cognitive overload. Our brains are not designed to process such vast amounts of information in short periods of time. This overload creates a state of mental exhaustion that can manifest as difficulty concentrating, feeling overwhelmed, and experiencing a diminished capacity to make decisions.

Emotional Exhaustion: The Toll of Never Fully Disconnecting and the Emotional Depletion It Causes

Emotional exhaustion is one of the hallmark symptoms of digital burnout, and it often stems from the inability to fully disconnect from the digital world. In today's hyper-connected environment, even when we are physically away from work or taking a break, we are rarely free from the pull of digital devices. Whether it's checking our smartphones for work-related updates, scrolling through social media, or responding to messages, the act of constantly being "on" emotionally drains us over time.

The mental and emotional toll of perpetual engagement with technology can result in feelings of disconnection and burnout. People who are unable to switch off from their devices often report feeling emotionally drained and disconnected from their surroundings. It becomes difficult to enjoy leisure time or spend meaningful moments with friends and family, as the compulsion to remain plugged in interferes with emotional recovery.

This emotional depletion manifests in various ways, from irritability and mood swings to a general sense of disillusionment with daily life. The inability to create emotional boundaries— such as establishing time for relaxation and personal activities without digital distractions—

contributes to a cycle of emotional exhaustion that becomes increasingly difficult to break.

Cognitive Decline: How Excessive Screen Time Affects Memory, Attention, and Focus

The effects of excessive screen time on cognitive functioning are profound, with studies showing that prolonged exposure to digital devices can negatively impact memory, attention, and focus. Continuous digital engagement—especially with fast-paced social media platforms—promotes multitasking, but multitasking actually decreases cognitive efficiency and impairs the brain's ability to concentrate.

When switching between tasks frequently (for example, responding to messages while reading an article or attending a video meeting), the brain is constantly "resetting" itself, which leads to a reduction in deep focus. This constant switching between different activities makes it harder to retain information and can lead to forgetfulness and difficulty concentrating.

Furthermore, excessive screen time has been linked to changes in the brain's structure. Research has shown that prolonged exposure to screens can affect the hippocampus, the part of the brain responsible for memory and learning. This impact on cognitive functioning can lead to a decrease in attention span, a diminished ability to focus on long-term goals, and difficulty retaining new information.

In addition to short-term memory issues, excessive screen time can also affect overall mental clarity. People who spend prolonged hours on digital devices often experience "brain fog," a state of mental fatigue that makes it challenging to think clearly or make decisions. This cognitive decline can exacerbate feelings of burnout, as individuals feel mentally worn out and unable to focus on important tasks.

Conclusion

The psychological impact of digital burnout extends far beyond feeling tired or stressed. It influences mental health, emotional well-being, and cognitive functioning, creating a complex web of challenges that require holistic approaches to overcome. As digital engagement continues to play a dominant role in our lives, it is essential to recognize and address the psychological consequences of this constant connectivity. By understanding these impacts, we can take the first steps toward reclaiming our mental, emotional, and cognitive health in an increasingly digital world.

Chapter 5: The Physical Effects of Digital Burnout

While the psychological and emotional consequences of digital burnout are well-documented, the physical effects of excessive digital engagement are equally significant. Our bodies were not designed to remain in constant contact with screens, and prolonged exposure to digital devices can have lasting consequences. This chapter delves into the physical toll of digital burnout, including sleep disruption, physical ailments, and overall fatigue.

Sleep Disruption: How Blue Light and Constant Screen Time Disrupt Sleep Patterns and Circadian Rhythms

One of the most immediate physical consequences of digital burnout is disrupted sleep. With the increasing prevalence of smartphones, tablets, and computers, more and more people are engaging with digital screens late into the night.

This constant screen time, especially before bed, has a direct impact on sleep quality due to the emission of blue light from digital devices.

Blue light, which is a high-energy visible light, is known to interfere with the production of melatonin, a hormone that regulates sleep. Melatonin signals to the body that it's time to rest, but blue light exposure during the evening suppresses this hormone, making it harder to fall asleep and stay asleep. As a result, individuals may experience difficulty winding down, leading to insomnia or poor-quality sleep.

The disruption of circadian rhythms—our natural sleep-wake cycles—can have a domino effect on physical and mental well-being. Chronic sleep deprivation resulting from late-night screen usage can contribute to mood disorders, weakened immune function, and impaired cognitive performance. Over time, poor sleep patterns caused by digital burnout may increase the risk of developing more serious health conditions, such as heart disease and diabetes.

Physical Ailments: Eye Strain, Headaches, Back Pain, and Carpal Tunnel Syndrome Due to Prolonged Digital Device Use

The extended use of digital devices is also associated with a range of physical ailments. One of the most common complaints is **digital eye strain**, often referred to as **computer vision syndrome**. Prolonged staring at screens can lead to symptoms such as dry eyes, blurred vision, and difficulty focusing. This eye strain occurs due to the constant need for the eyes to adjust to the brightness and focus on small text or images for long periods.

In addition to eye strain, headaches are a common physical consequence of digital burnout. The strain on the eyes from continuous screen time can trigger tension headaches or migraines, particularly in individuals who are already prone to these conditions. The bright, flickering light of digital screens can further exacerbate these issues, especially in low-light environments.

Posture-related issues are another concern for individuals who spend long hours in front of a screen. The typical hunched posture—often seen when people sit for extended periods looking at a laptop or smartphone—can lead to chronic **back and neck pain**. Over time, poor posture may result in long-term musculoskeletal problems, making it even more difficult for individuals to engage in physical activities or even perform daily tasks without discomfort.

Additionally, **carpal tunnel syndrome**, a condition caused by repetitive strain on the wrist, is increasingly common among those who spend extended periods typing or using touchscreens. This condition causes numbness, tingling, and pain in the hands and wrists, making it difficult for individuals to perform simple tasks without discomfort.

Fatigue and Low Energy: The Physical Manifestation of Digital Overload and Its Impact on Overall Health

Physical fatigue is one of the most common manifestations of digital burnout. While digital devices are designed to provide constant stimulation, the impact of this constant engagement can be exhausting. Extended exposure to screens and the mental overload that comes with it drain energy reserves and leave individuals feeling physically tired and sluggish.

People experiencing digital burnout often report a sense of "mental fatigue" that goes hand in hand with physical tiredness. The continuous mental effort required to process information, respond to messages, or stay engaged with social media can leave the body feeling drained. As a result, even basic tasks can feel overwhelming, and productivity can decline sharply.

This physical fatigue is compounded by the lack of physical activity that often accompanies excessive digital use. When people spend long hours sitting in front of a screen, they tend to become less active, leading to a decrease in overall physical health. Reduced movement can result in weight gain, muscle atrophy, and a general sense of low energy. Moreover, digital overload may contribute to poor eating habits, with individuals turning to unhealthy snacks or skipping meals due to a lack of time or energy.

Conclusion

The physical effects of digital burnout are far-reaching and can have long-lasting consequences on an individual's health. Sleep disruptions, eye strain, headaches, musculoskeletal pain, and fatigue are just some of the physical manifestations of our increasing dependence on technology. As our lives become more digitized, it is essential to prioritize self-care and set boundaries to mitigate these physical effects. By understanding the connection between digital overload and physical health, we can take the necessary steps to protect our bodies from the toll of constant digital engagement.

Chapter 6: The Impact on Relationships

As digital devices become more ingrained in our everyday lives, the toll on personal relationships has become increasingly apparent. While technology has brought about many conveniences, it has also created new barriers that affect how we connect with others. This chapter explores the negative impact of digital burnout on relationships, focusing on social isolation, family dynamics, and work-life balance.

Social Isolation: How Excessive Screen Time Leads to a Disconnect from Real-World Relationships

One of the most significant consequences of digital burnout is the growing sense of social isolation. Ironically, while technology is designed to keep us connected, excessive screen time often leads to a disconnect from real-world relationships. Many individuals spend hours engaging with virtual communities, whether through social media, gaming, or endless news feeds, leaving little time for face-to-face interactions.

This digital isolation can manifest in various ways. People may find themselves physically present in social settings, such as family gatherings or social events, but emotionally distant and preoccupied with their devices. The addiction to notifications and the compulsion to check screens constantly lead to diminished attention and empathy toward those around us. Over time, this erodes the quality of relationships and creates a sense of loneliness, even in the company of others.

Social isolation can also affect mental health, as the lack of in-person connections leaves individuals feeling unsupported. Real-world conversations and emotional bonds are essential for psychological well-being, and without these connections, feelings of loneliness, depression, and anxiety can intensify.

Family Dynamics: The Strain on Family Life, Particularly Between Parents and Children, Due to Digital Distractions

Family life has undergone a significant transformation in the digital age. While technology can offer opportunities for connection, it has also introduced new challenges, particularly when it comes to managing screen time within the household. Parents, in particular, find themselves balancing the demands of their professional and personal lives, often at the expense of quality family time.

Parents may become distracted by work emails or social media notifications while at home, leading to less engagement with their children. The constant digital distractions can result in missed moments—whether it's a family dinner, helping with homework, or having meaningful conversations. Children, in turn, may grow up accustomed to their parents' preoccupation with devices, leading to feelings of neglect or a lack of emotional connection.

The digital divide can also impact children's behavior. Excessive screen time, particularly with gaming or social media, has been linked to increased irritability, decreased attention span, and difficulty in developing interpersonal skills. The constant presence of devices at home may reduce face-to-face communication and foster an environment where technology takes precedence over human interaction.

Moreover, digital distractions can affect the way families manage household responsibilities and routines. Parents may struggle to set healthy boundaries around screen time, leading to family conflict and resentment. As the boundaries between work and home life blur, it becomes increasingly difficult for families to reconnect without the interference of screens.

Work-Life Balance: The Challenges of Managing Professional and Personal Life When Both Are Intertwined in the Digital Sphere

The blending of work and personal life due to digital devices has made it harder than ever to maintain a healthy work-life balance. With the advent of smartphones, laptops, and other connected devices, work can now follow us home, disrupting the time meant for relaxation or spending time with loved ones. The ability to constantly check emails, attend virtual meetings, or manage work tasks from anywhere has led to a culture of being "always on."

For many remote workers, this constant connectivity results in the inability to separate professional responsibilities from personal life. Even when not officially working, people feel compelled to respond to emails, messages, and calls, leading to stress, exhaustion, and reduced time for personal activities. This lack of boundaries erodes the distinction between work and leisure, resulting in burnout that affects both professional performance and personal well-being.

The digital age has also introduced new challenges to personal relationships. When work intrudes on family time—whether through late-night emails or early-morning conference calls—it can lead to frustration, conflict, and a sense of imbalance. Partners may feel neglected or resentful when one person is constantly preoccupied with work-related tasks, leaving little time for shared experiences or relaxation.

As digital tools continue to permeate both professional and personal spaces, achieving a true work-life balance requires intentional effort. Setting clear boundaries for when to unplug, establishing "tech-free" zones or times, and prioritizing in-person connections are essential for maintaining a healthy equilibrium between work and life.

Conclusion

The impact of digital burnout on relationships is profound and far-reaching. While technology can foster communication and connection, it also introduces new challenges in how we interact with others. From social isolation and strained family dynamics to the blending of work and personal life, the effects of digital overload on relationships are undeniable. By recognizing these impacts and taking proactive steps to mitigate the negative consequences of excessive screen time, individuals can preserve the quality of their relationships and restore balance to their lives.

Chapter 7: Reclaiming Your Time: Digital Detox Strategies

In a world that is constantly connected, taking control of our digital habits is more important than ever. The constant flow of information, notifications, and digital demands can quickly overwhelm us, leaving us feeling drained and disconnected. This chapter presents practical strategies for reclaiming your time and mental space, with a focus on mindful technology use, scheduled downtime, and learning the power of saying "no" to digital distractions.

Mindful Technology Use: Implementing Boundaries and Setting Intentional Limits on Screen Time

The first step toward reclaiming your time is becoming more mindful of how you use technology. Mindful technology use involves being intentional about the time spent on digital devices and the ways in which they impact your mental and emotional well-being.

Start by **setting boundaries** around when and where you engage with technology. For example, avoid checking work emails outside of office hours or setting specific times for social media usage. These boundaries help create a clear separation between personal and professional time and can help reduce the feeling of being "always on." Additionally, setting limits on screen time can be beneficial in preventing burnout. Many smartphones and apps now have built-in tools that allow you to monitor and limit usage, giving you more control over your digital habits.

When using digital devices, make a conscious effort to be present in the moment. For instance, instead of mindlessly scrolling through social media, focus on purposeful engagement, such as reading an article, catching up with friends, or researching a topic of interest. This mindful approach helps to combat the feeling of constant digital overwhelm and encourages a healthier, more fulfilling relationship with technology.

Scheduled Downtime: The Importance of Taking Regular Breaks from Digital Devices to Recharge

In the digital age, it's easy to fall into the trap of continuous screen time, whether for work, entertainment, or socializing. However, **scheduled downtime** is essential for mental and physical well-being. Regular breaks from digital devices allow you to recharge, focus on other aspects of your life, and reconnect with yourself and the world around you.

One of the most effective ways to incorporate downtime into your routine is to follow the **20-20-20 rule**: every 20 minutes, take a 20-second break by looking at something 20 feet away. This simple practice helps reduce eye strain and gives your brain a much-needed break from continuous digital engagement.

In addition to eye and mental rest, it's important to step away from screens for longer periods each day. This could involve taking breaks during work hours to go for a walk, engage in physical activity, or simply relax without any digital distractions. Scheduling regular tech-free times during your day—such as during meals, before bedtime, or on weekends—can provide significant relief from digital burnout. Use this time to engage in activities that bring joy, such as reading, spending time with family, pursuing hobbies, or enjoying nature.

By prioritizing regular breaks and scheduled downtime, you help reset your mind and body, making it easier to focus when you do engage with technology.

The Power of No: Learning to Say No to Digital Distractions and Unnecessary Online Commitments

In today's digital world, saying "yes" to everything can easily lead to burnout. Whether it's responding to every email, joining every online group, or keeping up with every social media trend, our digital lives are filled with distractions that drain our energy and attention. Learning to say **"no"** is a powerful tool for reclaiming your time and protecting your mental health.

Start by evaluating your digital commitments and responsibilities. Ask yourself which activities truly serve your personal and professional goals and which ones are simply adding to your stress. It's okay to step back from certain digital interactions, whether it's limiting time spent on non-urgent emails, unfollowing accounts that don't bring value, or turning down digital invitations that don't align with your priorities.

Saying no to digital distractions also means being more selective about where you invest your time online. For example, rather than spending hours scrolling through social media, choose to engage in more meaningful interactions, such as participating in online communities that align with your interests or values. If you're overwhelmed by constant digital notifications, consider using apps that block distractions or mute notifications for certain periods of the day.

Learning the power of no not only helps you take control of your time but also encourages a more focused, intentional, and mindful approach to digital engagement.

Conclusion

Reclaiming your time in the digital age requires intentional effort and a commitment to setting boundaries, taking breaks, and prioritizing meaningful engagement. By practicing **mindful technology use**, incorporating **scheduled**

downtime into your routine, and embracing the **power of no**, you can protect your mental and physical well-being from the constant barrage of digital distractions. These strategies help create a healthier relationship with technology, allowing you to enjoy its benefits while maintaining balance in your life.

Chapter 8: Building Healthy Digital Habits

In a world where digital technology often overwhelms us, establishing healthy digital habits is essential for maintaining mental, emotional, and physical well-being. This chapter explores three powerful strategies for building healthier relationships with technology: **digital minimalism, tech-free zones**, and **mindfulness practices**. By simplifying our digital consumption, creating spaces for disconnection, and incorporating mindfulness techniques, we can regain control over our digital lives and reduce the stress that comes with constant connectivity.

Digital Minimalism: Simplifying Digital Consumption and Focusing on Quality Rather Than Quantity

Digital minimalism is a mindset that encourages simplifying and decluttering our digital lives. Rather than mindlessly consuming information and spending time on digital platforms out of habit, digital minimalism focuses on **quality over quantity**. The goal is to streamline digital usage to what truly serves your personal and professional objectives, helping you minimize distractions and avoid digital overload.

Start by evaluating the digital tools, platforms, and content you engage with on a daily basis. Ask yourself: Which apps or websites add value to my life? Which ones drain my time and attention without providing meaningful benefits? By identifying these key areas, you can begin to eliminate unnecessary digital distractions.

For example, you might choose to unsubscribe from newsletters that clutter your inbox or unfollow social media accounts that don't align with your interests or values. Consider limiting your use of certain apps to specific time frames during the day or removing apps that contribute to mindless scrolling.

Digital minimalism also extends to your digital workspace. Consolidating tasks and organizing your files, emails, and apps can help you stay focused and reduce mental clutter. The goal is to focus on the essentials and eliminate the noise, allowing you to use technology in a more intentional and meaningful way.

By simplifying your digital consumption, you reduce the feeling of being overwhelmed and reclaim time and mental energy for other pursuits that matter more.

Tech-Free Zones: Designating Spaces and Times Where Technology Is Not Allowed to Interrupt

Creating **tech-free zones** is another powerful strategy for building healthier digital habits. These are designated spaces or times in your life where technology is intentionally excluded. Tech-free zones help you disconnect from the constant pull of digital devices and foster more mindful, present moments with yourself and others.

Consider implementing tech-free zones in your home, especially in areas where relaxation, family interaction, or personal time is meant to occur. For example, you could designate your bedroom as a **no-tech zone** to improve sleep quality by eliminating screen time before bed. Similarly, setting the dining table as a tech-free zone encourages more meaningful conversations during meals.

Establish tech-free times in your daily schedule as well. Consider having **phone-free hours**, such as during your morning routine, lunch breaks, or before bed, to give yourself a mental break from technology. Having these boundaries allows your mind and body to relax and recharge without the constant influx of notifications, messages, and digital distractions.

Tech-free zones create physical and mental spaces that encourage disconnection from digital devices, helping you focus on more important aspects of your life—whether that's personal reflection, spending quality time with loved ones, or engaging in activities that bring you joy and relaxation.

Mindfulness Practices: Techniques Such as Meditation, Journaling, and Deep Breathing to Reconnect with the Present Moment and Reduce the Stress of Constant Digital Engagement

Incorporating **mindfulness practices** into your daily routine is an effective way to counterbalance the stress and overwhelm that can result from excessive digital engagement. Mindfulness involves focusing on the present moment, letting go of distractions, and observing thoughts and feelings without judgment. By practicing mindfulness, you can reduce the mental clutter caused by constant digital consumption and reconnect with the present moment.

Here are some mindfulness practices that can help you reduce digital stress:

- **Meditation**: Practicing daily meditation helps calm the mind and alleviate the mental chatter that often comes with digital overload. Even a few minutes of deep breathing and focused attention can help you feel more grounded and present. You can use guided meditation apps or simply focus on your breath and sensations in your body.
- **Journaling**: Writing in a journal can be a powerful tool for managing stress and gaining clarity. Journaling allows you to reflect on your digital habits, identify sources of stress, and set intentions for improving your relationship with technology. You can use a journal to write

about your experiences, thoughts, and feelings related to your digital usage.

- **Deep Breathing**: Deep breathing exercises, such as **box breathing** (inhale for four counts, hold for four counts, exhale for four counts, hold for four counts), can quickly reduce stress and improve mental focus. Practicing deep breathing when you feel overwhelmed by digital distractions can help calm your nervous system and bring you back to the present moment.

Mindfulness practices also support emotional regulation, allowing you to handle the stress of digital engagement more effectively. By integrating mindfulness into your daily routine, you can become more aware of your digital habits and develop greater control over when and how you engage with technology.

Conclusion

Building healthy digital habits is essential for maintaining balance in an increasingly digital world. By embracing **digital minimalism**, creating **tech-free zones**, and incorporating **mindfulness practices**, you can reclaim your time, reduce stress, and cultivate a more intentional relationship with technology. These strategies allow you to reduce digital overload, promote mental clarity, and create space for more meaningful and present moments in your life.

Chapter 9: Rebuilding Emotional Resilience

In the aftermath of digital burnout, rebuilding emotional resilience is crucial for recovery and long-term well-being. Emotional resilience is the ability to adapt to and recover from difficult situations, challenges, or stressors, and it plays a key role in overcoming the effects of digital overload. This chapter focuses on self-care strategies that promote emotional well-being and recovery from burnout, including physical activities, nature walks, and hobbies.

Self-Care Strategies: Activities That Promote Emotional Well-Being and Recovery from Burnout

Self-care is essential for rebuilding emotional resilience, especially when recovering from the exhaustion and stress caused by digital burnout. When we neglect our emotional needs in the midst of constant connectivity, our mental health can deteriorate, leaving us feeling drained, overwhelmed, and disconnected from ourselves. To foster resilience and rebuild emotional strength, it's important to engage in activities that nourish both the mind and body.

1. Exercise: A Powerful Tool for Restoring Energy and Resilience

Regular physical activity is one of the most effective ways to improve emotional well-being and promote recovery from burnout. Exercise releases **endorphins**, the body's natural "feel-good" hormones, which help reduce stress, anxiety, and depression. It also promotes **better sleep**, boosts **energy levels**, and enhances overall mood.

Consider incorporating activities like walking, jogging, cycling, swimming, or yoga into your daily routine. Engaging in physical exercise not only improves your physical health but also provides a much-needed break from screens and technology. Whether it's a vigorous workout or a calming stretch, exercise helps reset your mind and body, making it a critical part of your recovery journey.

You don't need to commit to intense workout routines right away. Start small with a few minutes of activity each day, and gradually increase the duration and intensity. This consistent practice will build your emotional resilience, making it easier to cope with stress and digital burnout.

2. Nature Walks: Reconnecting with the Outdoors

Spending time in nature is a highly restorative activity that can alleviate the symptoms of digital burnout and promote emotional healing. Nature has a unique ability to soothe the mind and reduce stress by engaging our senses in a calming and grounding way. Whether it's a leisurely walk through a local park, hiking in the mountains, or simply sitting near a body of water, immersing yourself in nature helps you unplug from the digital world and reconnect with the present moment.

Research has shown that exposure to nature can improve mood, reduce anxiety, and increase feelings of relaxation. The natural environment encourages mindfulness, which helps shift your focus away from the constant stream of information that contributes to burnout.

Aim to spend time outdoors regularly, even if it's just for a few minutes each day. Take a walk in the park during lunch breaks, go for a nature hike on weekends, or sit outside with a cup of tea while listening to the sounds of birds or wind in the trees. These moments of connection with nature can provide a sense of peace and clarity that supports emotional recovery.

3. Hobbies and Creative Outlets: Rediscovering Passion and Purpose

Engaging in hobbies and creative activities is another powerful strategy for rebuilding emotional resilience. Hobbies that bring you joy and fulfillment help distract you from digital stressors and provide a sense of purpose and accomplishment. Whether it's painting, knitting, gardening, playing a musical instrument, or writing, creative outlets allow you to express yourself and tap into your inner sense of creativity.

Taking time for hobbies also promotes **mindfulness**, as these activities often require your full attention, helping you disengage from digital distractions and reconnect with your senses. When you immerse yourself in something you love, it can be incredibly healing, allowing you to focus on the present moment and reduce the mental overload caused by technology.

If you haven't explored a hobby in a while, now is the perfect time to rediscover something that excites you. If you're unsure where to start, think about activities that once brought you joy or explore new interests. Hobbies give you an opportunity to focus on what makes you happy, boosting your emotional resilience as you recover from burnout.

4. Practicing Gratitude: Shifting Your Focus Toward Positivity

In addition to physical activities and hobbies, cultivating a **gratitude practice** is another important self-care strategy for rebuilding emotional resilience. Gratitude helps shift your focus away from digital frustrations and burnout, encouraging you to appreciate the positive aspects of your life, no matter how small.

Each day, take a moment to reflect on three things you're grateful for. These can range from meaningful relationships to small moments of joy, such as a warm cup of coffee in the morning or the feeling of sunshine on your face. By consciously acknowledging what's going well in your life, you cultivate a mindset of resilience and positivity that can help you navigate the challenges of digital burnout.

Gratitude encourages emotional strength and perspective, reminding you that even in times of stress, there are aspects of your life that bring you joy and fulfillment.

5. Meditation and Deep Breathing: Calming the Mind and Restoring Balance

Finally, incorporating **meditation** and **deep breathing** exercises into your daily routine can help you manage stress and rebuild emotional resilience. Meditation allows you to clear your mind, center yourself, and regain mental clarity, while deep breathing exercises help reduce the physiological symptoms of stress, such as rapid heart rate and shallow breathing.

You don't need to meditate for long periods of time—just five to ten minutes of focused breathing or guided meditation can significantly reduce stress and improve your ability to manage digital overload. Apps like Headspace or Calm can guide you through short meditation sessions designed to relieve stress and increase emotional resilience.

Conclusion

Rebuilding emotional resilience after experiencing digital burnout requires a holistic approach to self-care. By incorporating **exercise**, **nature walks**, **hobbies**, **gratitude**, and **mindfulness practices**, you can gradually recover from the emotional toll of constant digital engagement. These self-care strategies help restore balance, promote emotional well-being, and empower you to navigate the challenges of the digital age with greater strength and clarity.

By consistently nurturing your emotional health, you'll be better equipped to manage the stresses of technology and regain control over your life, allowing you to thrive both personally and professionally.

Conclusion: Reclaiming Balance in the Digital Age

In the age of constant connectivity, digital burnout has become an undeniable challenge for individuals across the globe. As we navigate the overwhelming demands of our digital lives, it is easy to lose sight of the importance of balance and self-care. The relentless barrage of notifications, emails, and social media updates can leave us feeling mentally, emotionally, and physically drained. Yet, as we have explored throughout this book, there is hope. Through conscious effort and intentional action, we can reclaim our time, restore our energy, and rebuild our emotional resilience.

The strategies outlined in this book, from digital detoxes and mindful technology use to the power of self-care, emotional resilience, and healthy digital habits, provide a roadmap for regaining control over our digital lives. It's essential to recognize that while technology has undoubtedly transformed the way we live and work, it is not without its consequences. By making space for **boundaries**, **downtime**, and **self-reflection**, we can start to mitigate the effects of digital burnout and embrace a healthier, more balanced relationship with technology.

The journey toward recovery may not be immediate, and the challenges of a hyper-connected world will continue to persist. However, by implementing the tools and practices discussed in this book, we can build emotional strength, foster deeper connections with ourselves and others, and navigate the digital landscape with greater mindfulness and intention.

As we move forward, let us remember that we have the power to create a life where technology serves us, not the other way around. Reclaiming balance is not about rejecting technology altogether but about using it in a way that enhances our lives rather than detracts from our well-being. By embracing flexibility, cultivating self-awareness, and prioritizing our health, we can rise above the pressures of the digital age and live lives that are not only productive but also fulfilling.

The key to thriving in a digitally-driven world lies in the conscious choices we make. So, take the first step today. Disconnect, recharge, and begin the journey toward a more balanced, healthier, and more intentional life.

www.ingramcontent.com/pod-product-compliance
Lightning Source LLC
LaVergne TN
LVHW051608050326
832903LV00033B/4412